Silent Cries

Silent Cries

LANDY PEREZ FELICIANO

Library of Congress Control Number:		2020917479
ISBN:	Softcover	978-1-5065-3406-0
	eBook	978-1-5065-3407-7

Print information available on the last page.

Rev. date: 18/11/2020

To order additional copies of this book, contact:
Palibrio
1663 Liberty Drive, Suite 200
Bloomington, IN 47403
Toll Free from the U.S.A 877.407.5847
Toll Free from Mexico 01.800.288.2243
Toll Free from Spain 900.866.949
From other International locations +1.812.671.9757
Fax: 01.812.355.1576
orders@palibrio.com
813061

contents

INTRODUCTION

first comes love

First comes love, then comes marriage
then comes….

This book is for women of all walks of life who are going through the hard and lonely road of infertility. You are loved, you are cherished, and most importantly, you are not alone. My hope is that after reading *Silent Cries*, you find comfort in the One who understands you - God.

It is also for the men who are on the same, deeply emotional road. After all, it takes two to make one. Your ambitions of fatherhood and legacy are also suffering. A man's first thought is typically to be supportive, to be the strong husband, the shoulder to cry on…but who tends to you? The truth is most men don't know how to properly be supportive because they cannot find the words to express how they feel. And most women are so wrapped up in their struggle that they forget their mate is also going through it as well.

When this issue is not handled with love, patience, and understanding, it leads to blame, anger, regret, and bitterness. Today, I want you to believe that God has a better life for you.

You will be challenged to view your journey for what it is...*your* journey. This will free you from any comparisons that might be lingering. We all envision the perfect, white picket-fenced family, until we step into their house and realize that they live a less-than-perfect life. Everyone is struggling with something, whether they choose to publicly display it or not. It's time to stop feeling sorry for yourself and be unapologetic about your situation, because regardless of the outcome, God has a beautiful and perfect plan for your life and for that of your family.

My friend, you are an inspiration to the masses, and you don't even know it. But after reading this book, you will understand that there is a greater purpose in you, and that your journey is simply the vehicle that will propel you into your destiny.

a voice that cries

Many times, I would cry myself to sleep
Thinking, "What is wrong with me?"
Why am I barren
When I possess so much love
And I simply want to share it
With my own children
Flesh of my flesh
And bone of my bone
I want to be blessed
With the gift of motherhood
And experience the unexplainable joy
Of bringing a child into this world.
I want to finally take a test
And have it be positive
Without the worries of it being false again
I wonder what my sonogram would be
Will the baby look like him or me?
Call me crazy
But I think it would be amazing
To experience it all,
The morning sickness
And the sleepless nights

The daily kicks and the waddle walks
I want to determine
If the body pillow really works or not
And not just hear it from everyone else
Planning my baby shower would be so much fun
I've had the vision for a long time
I just need a baby in the bun
Registering at Target or Baby's R Us seem to be the places for moms
So, I guess that would be my new stop
I want to know what Braxton Hicks are
And experience the labor pains
I don't care if I have the epidural or not
It won't make me less of a woman
I just want to be a mother
The biggest reward
Is to have my baby in my arms
To love, care and comfort
I'm looking forward
To nights of sleep deprivation
And of constant feedings.
Because it will be a daily reminder
Of my miracle healing.
Don't talk to me about breast milk or formulas or vaccinations or side effects
Speak life into me
Speak life into my children
I'll cross that bridge when I get there
But in the meantime, help me get there
With your words of encouragement and kindness
Don't assume I don't want kids
Of course, I do
Don't be so straight forward
And ask me what I am waiting for
Don't tell me, time is ticking

I've been watching my biological clock for a minute
And I know I'm down to the wire
So, please don't add fuel to the fire
I don't need added pressure
From people who don't know my story
I have a medical condition
That I have no control over
If it were up to me
I would have two toddlers
A baby boy and a daughter
Filling my life with joy and laughter
But it's out of my hands
And in the hands of my Creator
Please be considerate and be nice
I have my days and I have my nights
Pregnancy announcements and baby showers are not easy
Please believe me when I say,
I am happy for you and your family
I'm just sad because my husband and I feel alone
Without the presence of our own little ones
Infertility is dark and painful
However, I am forever grateful
Because I can be a voice
For so many women who are silently crying out for help
On behalf of us,
Help us by being there
Show us your love and care
Help us by being genuine and kind
My struggle is not yours
And your struggle is not mine
However, together we will overcome
Anything that comes our way
Let's remind each other
That we are stronger together
And united as sisters, we are better.

CHAPTER ONE
---

silent cries

It was a Wednesday morning when my husband and I received the dreaded news, the words a couple never want to hear. "I'm sorry, you can't have children." I remember everything so vividly, as if it were a few minutes ago. I remember the feeling of disbelief, all the positive thinking quickly melting away into a pool of despair. How could this be possible? I thought to myself. "Are you sure doctor? There must be a mistake. We're both healthy."

"Yes, I am sure." replied the doctor, showing me the evidence of the tests that were performed. As I sat in his office, his words began to echo further and further away as I gazed into space, wanting someone to pinch me so I could wake up from this terrible dream. But it wasn't a dream. That day I began to live a reality I never imagined I would have to face – infertility specialists, treatments, surgeries, procedures, oral medication, injections, paperwork – you name it, I did it. Over the next couple of years, this became my new normal.

That Wednesday morning, after we walked away from the doctor's office, my husband and I cried together in our car, believing God for a miracle. We believed His report over our lives which was to be fruitful and multiply. Little did we know that this day would be the start of a long, painful, and lonely road ahead. Our faith was tested and on many occasions our marriage was tested as well. We had so many questions and no answers. That day, God's silence began to unfold in such a way that it was deafening. In such a crucial time of life, when I needed to hear from Him the most, I heard the least. I quickly realized that my husband and I were both entering a season of silence, where we would have to learn to be patient and hear God's voice above everyone else's.

A Moment of Silence

After writing my first book, A Moment of Silence, I began to experience an unexpected moment of silence in my life. To be honest with you, when I wrote it, I was in a good place. I had a loving husband, and still do, a supportive family, great friends, and an amazing church family. Life was great! I remember thinking to myself, "How am I going to respond to people when they ask me, 'Landy, what inspired you to write "A Moment of Silence"'? What are you going to say?"

My mind would always backtrack to the days of single hood, where I had to wait a little longer than most women for marriage. I thought *that* was my moment of silence! I thought, "Yes Lord, that sounds like a great answer – single hood." Afterall, that season in my life inspired me to write the book, right?! However, little did I know that I was about to embark on a journey that would test me even greater than that former season. My bright days were about to turn into my darkest nights. I began to live nights of profound anguish and unbearable pain. Loneliness and abandonment became my daily companions, creating a constant vocabulary of "Why God? Why me?" Yes, this was coming from the same person who wrote the book, *A Moment of Silence: God Wants to Speak to You.* I was the one who encouraged her readers to believe that, despite their troubles, God was trustworthy.

You see, Christian clichés look great on paper, but when it is time to live them, it becomes a different story. I now had to practice what I was preaching. My biggest frustration was that God was not speaking to me when I needed Him the most. It was almost as if He was saying, "Peace out!" leaving me alone to figure it out. Although, I know that is not true at all; your feelings and emotions can be very deceiving and overpowering. So many questions flooded my mind, oceans of tears seemed to drown my faith, and silent cries took place during the darkest hour of my life. I didn't understand how or why, but there was purpose in my pain. There was a moment of silence where God was not speaking to me, or so it seemed. But I was greatly mistaken, as He was speaking loud and clear – I just wasn't listening.

Be Your Way

How many times do we find ourselves searching for answers, pleading with God to speak to us a certain way? Too many to count! The problem is not whether God will speak; He always does. The issue is *how* will He do it. Man, we can be so stubborn at times, just like the Burger King commercial, "Have It Your Way." We always want to have it our way. What's fascinating is that Burger King decided to ditch their motto of over forty years to a more personal motto of "Be Your Way." Burger King released a statement in 2014 that the new motto was intended to remind people that *They can and should live how they want anytime. It's ok to not be perfect ... Self-expression is most important and it's our differences that make us individuals instead of robots.*" Fernando Machado, Burger King's senior vice president of global brand management, noticed in an interview that "Have It Your Way" focuses only on the purchase – the ability to customize a burger. By contrast, he said, "Be Your Way" is about making a connection with a person's greater lifestyle.

The problem with the "Be Your Way" attitude is that we think we know what we want, but really, we don't. The more options we are presented with, the more indecisive we become. For instance, say you go through a fast food drive-through; unless you are familiar with the menu, it will often take you a minute or two to decide what to order. By nature, we are indecisive human beings. We are always changing our minds. My husband does that a lot, especially with clothing! I have a system at home where every night, I pick out my clothes for the next day and for me that works; it's one less thing for me to worry about in the morning. It seems logical, doesn't it? Apparently, not for most people, my husband included. Every morning he picks out his clothes and irons them before going to work. I don't understand why anyone would waste their time doing that in the morning. His response is, "I change my mind a lot!" And I must agree. I've witnessed him picking his clothes the night before and then the next morning, he's just not in the mood to wear them. So, he goes back into the closet and chooses something different. I'm like that sometimes. However, most of the time I stick to my guns.

Because we are complicated beings, we cannot have it our way. Things cannot be your way, they cannot be my way, they must be God's way! He knows best. The Bible says in James 1:17 that *"Every good and perfect gift is from above, coming down from the Father of the heavenly lights, who does not change like shifting shadows."* Psalm 102:27 says, *"But you remain the same and your years will never end."* Hebrews 13:8 says that, *"Jesus Christ is the same yesterday and today and forever."* We don't know what we want, but God knows what we need. Although we are constantly changing our minds, God never does. That is why we should always say, "Lord, let my life *be your way* and not mine."

Your heavenly Father knows you better than anyone else. He created you in His image and knit you in your mother's womb. He knows your deepest desires! Moreover, He is not punishing you because you are not presently able to conceive. As difficult as this may sound, trust Him! His plans are bigger than you could ever imagine. Not a day goes wasted in God's eyes. While we see the years going by and the "biological clock" ticking, know that God doesn't operate on our timetable. He is never too early; He is never too late. Surrender your ways and allow Him to have His way in your life.

Silent Cries

Silent Cries – we have all had our share of them. They are not merely the visible tears that we cry, nor are they tears of happiness. They are not the type of tears that you can shed on someone's shoulders while they are telling you that everything will be alright. These are the inward tears that erupt like an avalanche, regardless of how strong and happy you are on the outside. Silent cries are the tears we pour out in private while exhibiting public joy. It is the pain that no one sees and the anguish no one hears. We can easily despise them because they take us to a place of vulnerability. Oh, how I know them very well!

Those were the types of emotions I began to experience right after the success of my first book. I thought, "Yes, we all go through tough times. But I will bounce right back, just as I have in the past." Everyone goes through moments of silence in their lives. I just thought that because it was me, my moment of silence would end a lot sooner than I anticipated. But let me tell you something: God is not impressed by what you may do or say! He will keep you in the fire for as long as needed, because only He knows when the right time is to come out.

Another thing I learned is that God is near. He is closer than we think, and He hears our cries, even if it seems like He doesn't. Psalms 34:18 says that, "*The Lord is close to the brokenhearted and saves those who are crushed in spirit.*" Never allow your problem to overshadow the promise that God has made you; the minute you do that, you slowly begin to lose hope and start to question God's spoken word over your life. Do not allow doubt and fear to take charge of your mind, because you will find yourself buried in discouragement and you'll begin to ask yourself repeatedly, "Will it ever end? Will this pain ever cease? Will great things ever happen for me? Will I ever see God's promises come to pass in my life, not after twenty years, not after I die, but soon?" You see, the strong faith you used to experience, which is now wavering, is being tested in the face of adversity. The question is, will you pass the test?

There is a quote that I have made my own over the years: "There can't be a testimony without a test." In this time of testing that you might be enduring, God is that professor who watches over you in the same way that a teacher watches over the students. And as a caring teacher, He will not speak while the test is underway, because He must allow you to finish. Rest assured; His silence does not mean He is not in the room!

You must believe that absolutely nothing gets past Him. It does not matter how dark and lonely your moment has been, you are not alone. Even though you have felt like God has been distant, I can assure you that He has remained closer to you than anyone has ever been. He has given you the necessary tools in order to pass the test. He has taken His time to teach you everything you need to know to move on to the next level. All you need to do is remember the lessons and remember His Word. It is in those moments of silence that you must anchor yourself to the Word of God, to His promises, to the words He has spoken over you, because His Word is what will sustain you in times of uncertainty. His Word is life.

Silent Reflection

Lord, I know that I have a shoulder to cry on when I need it the most. The Bible says that you gather up all my tears and store them. I thank you for hearing my cry, even when they are silent cries. When the pain is too much to bear and I cannot utter the words, I know that you know exactly what I am saying. Thank you for being my comforter and most importantly, for being by my side, even in those moments of excruciating silence. I know that you are working everything out for my good. This is why I am asking you to have it *your way*. Even when I don't understand what is going on in my life, I love you and I trust that you have a better plan for me. Let your will be done.

CHAPTER TWO

purpose in pain

It didn't matter how much I prayed, or how many times I stayed overnight at church vigils. It didn't matter how many people laid hands on me in prayer, or how many Bible verses I memorized, or even how much encouragement or wise counsel I received; God wasn't going to break His silence just because I wanted Him to. He would do it when the time was right. With each passing day, His silence would intensify, and the pain would become a little less bearable. I failed to realize that God was present during my pain, and His purpose would be made clear in my life, not today, not tomorrow, but in His perfect timing.

At the time, it was extremely hard to comprehend why God was allowing this to happen. It is not like I was being selfish, wanting riches to splurge, and to travel the world. My deepest desire was more profound than any riches man could ever attain – I yearned to be a mother. I wanted more than anything to make my husband a father and continue his and our legacy. I wanted to bear a seed inside of me that represented our union and our love for one another. You may feel the same way I did; in fact, I know you do because as women, we long to wake up that maternal instinct that lies within. Even if we are not mothers yet, we are able to direct that instinct to one thing or another. Don't just bury it or continue to let it sleep, shake it and wake it because it was placed within you for a reason, and God wants you to use it so that He can do something wonderful.

"I don't have a child" you may say. I get it. I don't have one either. As I am writing this chapter, I am speaking life into my situation, making a choice not to stay defeated in my misery. You see dear friend, you have a choice; you can either give up, stay stuck and feel sorry for yourself, or choose to have a radically different outlook. You have the choice to get up, dust yourself off and continue to move forward with a positive attitude, knowing that God is in control of your life, not doctors, treatments, or even yourself – He has the last word!

There must come a point in your life where you find yourself at a crossroads, where boys are separated from men, and girls from women. It is that moment where you must decide to either wallow in this situation until it consumes you or take a stand and put your faith into action. Yes, medically speaking, fertility may be impossible, but you have absolutely nothing to lose if you decide to put your faith into action. What was I going to do? What are *you* going to do?

As for me, being born and raised in the church, I have heard thousands of messages throughout my lifetime. I have spoken life into so many people in need and have seen the power of God manifested in so many lives. I have even seen miracles in my family. So, why wouldn't I believe God for a miracle in *my* life? The Bible says that

Jesus is the same yesterday, today, and forever. The same power that raised our Lord Jesus Christ from the dead, lives in us. Jesus said that we would do more in His name than what He did on the earth. He can do anything! And I have had to remind myself of His living power. You see, sometimes we get so consumed in our struggles that we magnify the problem instead of magnifying the power of God. The ball is in *your* court. I know it hurts, I know it's frustrating, I also know it's unfair. But we do not have control over what life throws at us; we only have control over how we react to it.

Sister Sister

My sister and I practically grew up as twins. We are fifteen months apart and have done everything together. We even got married together. You heard that correctly! We had a double wedding. It was her dream for us to tie the knot together and thankfully, our husbands agreed. It was a magically, perfect day. As the older sister, it was expected for me to get pregnant first; at the very least, for both of us to be pregnant together. However, it did not happen that way, as God had other plans. Two and half years into the marriage, my sister gave me the news that she was expecting. To be honest, she was a bit sad because she had always wanted me to get pregnant first, but I was so happy for her.

Her first born, named Joel, came into this world fully loved, especially by his auntie. In a sense, my maternal instincts awoken, and I became like a second mom to him. Three years later and still childless, I continue to feel that way. That is why I say it does not matter if you're not a mom; you can still feel maternal affection toward others, like your nieces and nephews. What's amazing is that I see a little bit of myself in them.

I have also become a spiritual mother for many of the youth in my church, praying for them, counseling them, worrying for them, just as a mother would. Don't wait until you receive what you are waiting for to begin doing what you are supposed to do. A child is a blessing and God entrust parents with such a great responsibility. Think about the people who God has entrusted to you. Who are you speaking life into? Who are you encouraging? Who are you raising up, spiritually speaking? It's all about perspective! When your outlook changes, you will see that you're surrounded by blessings. And when God finds you working, and not sitting around lamenting over the things you don't have, but doing your very best with what you do have, then He will surprise you with His very best.

In times of difficulty, it is important to understand that there is a greater plan, that your struggle is producing more than you realize. There is purpose in your pain. God is preparing you in the face of adversity so that you will become stronger than before. What was supposed to destroy you will be used as divine strength to walk in boldness and not in fear. In those moments of despair, hold steadfast and know that there must be more; God is working it all out for you. Your pain is the catalyst for your purpose, as it is precisely the steppingstone to the place where God wants to take you.

Until now, everything that you've gone through in life has not been accidental. Even your biggest mistakes and your deepest regrets have propelled you to this exact time and place. Absolutely nothing in life has gone to waste, for there is purpose behind every disappointment, every emotion, and every decision you have ever taken. Relieve yourself of the "what ifs." Yes, things may have played out differently than expected, but you are here now, and God's purpose will still be fulfilled in your life, regardless of the past.

When we fix our eyes on Jesus and not the circumstances, we begin to trust Him for everything. Even if we are in the middle of a terrible storm, if our eyes are locked on the Problem Solver instead of the problem, then we will be in good shape. I am reminded of the story of Peter when he walked on water. It's an amazing account of great faith and bravery. And although Peter is highly criticized for his lack of faith, his shortcomings just show how "human" he was. He was no different than us. The Bible says that Peter was in a boat in the middle of a great storm when Jesus approached him from the middle of the sea. Jesus told him to get out of the boat and walk toward him. Now, let me remind you that Peter was just as human as you or I. And having lived in Florida all my life, I know a thing or two about severe thunderstorms and hurricanes – it is nothing to take lightly! Yet, Peter obeyed the command of his Master, got out of the boat, and began walking on the water toward Jesus. Because his eyes were fixed on the Lord, he was able to keep walking in the supernatural. As soon as he took his eyes off Jesus, he began to sink. When we take our eyes off our problem-solving Savior, it will be the moment we begin to sink. However, if we manage to keep our eyes fixed on the One who can do all things, then we will be okay, and will manage to walk over our difficulties instead of drowning beneath them.

Raw + Real

Can I be totally transparent right now? As I am revising this chapter, I am reminded of the many things that have happened since I began. I can vividly remember the moment I wrote *Sister Sister*. It was a peaceful day in the month of September, and I was on the beautiful island of Puerto Rico with my husband. It was my first trip to the island, and I was just soaking it all in. I purposely took my laptop so that I could take advantage of a great opportunity to write. This happened three years ago. At this time, I was sure I would become pregnant, and that my baby would come not far behind my nephews. I now have a total of nine nieces and nephews from my siblings. And three years later, I am still waiting.

Much of what I've experienced during this three-year period has made me want to give up on writing this book. You will never know how many times I had the urge to just delete this manuscript and go on with my life as though this was never supposed to happen. You see, I wanted a fairytale ending. I wanted to have my baby in my hands and show you how miraculous a child's life really is. I wanted to testify of God's healing in my body and encourage you to keep believing Him for your miracle, because it is possible. And although I still believe this with all my heart, I wanted you to see the miracle in my life so that I could show you tangible evidence of God's goodness. I would have loved to include a series of pictures highlighting my journey to motherhood within this book. I had it all planned out! But as usual, God's plans do not typically align with what we have in mind.

So, yes! This book should have been completed a long time ago; but for three years, I closed my laptop, and suspended all writing indefinitely. Although I wanted a miracle in my hands, God was demanding the use of my hands for other reasons – to write for you! I mean, who can wrestle with God? You can resist but for a moment; and yet, He wins every single time! Three years later, I find myself in a new season and in a new decade. And although my circumstances have not changed, I believe that God allowed me to experience these things to teach me some valuable lessons necessary for my maturity. Consequently, my experiences can now help many women and men who are on a similar journey.

Silent Reflection

Patience and faith go hand-in-hand. Throughout Scripture we see the two together. What happens as we walk these out is called *process*. And we all must go through the process. Even though it hurts, and is painful, in the end, it will yield great results. Take a moment and thank God for your pain because He is up to something. The Bible says in Psalm 30:5 that weeping may endure for a night, but joy comes in the morning. Rejoice in the Lord because joy is coming. You will rise above the water and overcome the storms in your life. Rejoice because there is purpose in your pain.

CHAPTER THREE

---

shh... just listen

Many times, I thought my moment of silence would come to an end. Finally, God would respond! But things didn't work out that way, as God's moment to speak had not yet arrived. The days and months grew into years of waiting. I won't lie, I had good days and many more bad days. There were days when my faith went through the roof, and *nothing* was impossible. I was a mountain-mover, knowing God would do miracles in my life. And yet, there were days when I felt so lonely and defeated, I didn't want to talk to anyone or leave my room for anything. I wanted to be alone and wallow in my sorrow. I went through a painfully draining process, physically and emotionally. As the author of "A Moment of Silence," I was still experiencing profound silence in my life. It was deafening.

Located in the Mahalangur mountain range of Nepal, Mount Everest is the highest in the world, at a staggering 29,029 feet. Sometimes, my faith felt as though it was

30,000 feet high – there was no stopping me! I believed that God would make a way where there was no way. I was obedient to the Scriptures which commanded me to wait patiently. They declared that if I had the faith of a mustard seed, I could move any mountain in my way. However, God had other plans. My faith was being tested as He had not broken His silence. I was still waiting for my answer.

And as time passed, I came to realize that there was more to the silence than what I could have ever imagined. God was indeed speaking to me through His non-verbal expressions. His message was loud and clear; however, it was communicated in a way I did not yet know. My expectations for how He would speak did not allow me to hear correctly. I was putting God's ability to communicate with me in a box, one which I could control. Nevertheless, He was teaching me that He does what He wants, how He wants to do it. You may find yourself in a similar situation, expecting answers. You've prayed, pleaded, asked, believed, and are waiting to receive. But you find yourself disappointed time and time again. How do you get to the point where you start listening during the silence?

The answer begins by calming yourself down, putting aside your frustrations, and quieting your soul so that you can listen. You will begin to hear a word that whispers into your spirit. Clarity will never be found in the middle of chaos; it arrives when peace abides. In John 14:27 (AMP), Jesus says, *"Peace I leave with you: My [own] peace I now give...to you. Not as the world gives do I give to you. Do not let your hearts be troubled, neither let them be afraid. [Stop allowing yourselves to be agitated and disturbed; and do not permit yourselves to be fearful and intimidated and cowardly and unsettled.]"* God wants us to experience His special peace, not the kind of peace the world gives. His peace surpasses all understanding.

It's a peace that does not come from the world but from Jesus Himself. This means that our peace should not be robbed by the circumstances that occur in our lives. God does not want us to live a life of frustration, but one where His peace overshadows the chaos that overwhelms us.

After countless false pregnancy tests and failed infertility treatments, I had a decision to make. I was either going to allow frustration to completely take over my life, my mood, and my emotions, or I was going to surrender to, and continue trusting God's plan for my life. I came to the realization that there was more to God's silence than what I thought. He was actually trying to capture my attention with a clear message. However, I was too caught up in my problems, trying to fix them, throwing hissy fits and complaining about how unfair my life was. This resulted in me missing the big picture.

God was telling me, "Landy, shh… just listen." I heard Him telling me that there was a bigger purpose in store. It was more than just an infertility issue; this was simply the vehicle that He was allowing to fulfill His plan. I began to quiet down and really listen to what He was speaking. It was then that things began to make sense. I began to experience God's peace in such an incredible way, because I understood that He was still in control. As I heard Him speaking in this "silent" language, I began to understand what He was saying and doing.

Standing Faith

Did you know that there are over three thousand promises in the Bible that belong to us? As children of God, we are their rightful owners. The problem is that many of us do not take possession of them, and so oftentimes we miss out on the many blessings our

Heavenly Father has prepared for us. In Ephesians 6:14, we are advised to stand firm and hold our ground. This chapter speaks on the importance of bearing the armor of God, because we are in a battle and need the proper attire in order to become victorious. To "stand firm" is to be in position regardless of what is going on around us. Just think of the men and women in uniform. They are so focused on the task in front of them that nothing will distract them from completing the mission. This takes great discipline and determination and is not obtained overnight.

Someone who is standing firm will not be shaken by their circumstances, and their thoughts will not waver from the truth. I believe that we are all on this journey. Although some have mastered it more than others, everyone will be tested! For it is in these moments when we must engage in battle, that we can be shaken to the core. So, how can we remain strong when everything around us is shaking? The answer is *the Word of God*. Psalms 112:7 says, *"They do not fear bad news; they confidently trust the Lord to care for them."* I love this because although it does not say that bad news will not come, we will approach the challenges differently. We will remain calm, confidently trusting in the Lord who cares for and protects us.

Don't get me wrong! I still have my weak days. God hasn't showed me the entire picture for my life. I've just seen glimpses of what He is doing in me. And as of now, I am still waiting for my miracle. However, the big difference is that I am in control of my feelings. This does not mean I never have a sad thought, like when I hear of a pregnancy announcement from someone I know. You see, I have the power either to feed those thoughts that lead into a dark place, or I can choose to have peace and joy despite what my surroundings may dictate.

In 2 Corinthians 10:5, the Bible says that, *"We destroy arguments and every lofty opinion raised against the knowledge of God, and take every thought captive to obey Christ."* We are to take wrong thinking captive, confronting those thoughts with the Word of God. Any thought that does not conform to the thinking of the Gospel must be taken captive and brought to the obedience of Christ. We must do this because the mind is a battlefield where we are bombarded every single day, hour, and minute, with positive and negative information. If we are not able to filter the positive information from the negative, the enemy will have a field day with us. In Joyce Meyer's book, "The Battlefield of the Mind," she says, *"I believe many people think they don't have a choice about their thoughts. But you can think on purpose – positive thoughts or negative thoughts. If a negative thought comes into your head, you can cast it down and begin to renew your mind with the Word of God."*

I am not talking about a humanistic approach to positive thinking; I am referring to a Bible-based, Word of God type of thinking. We must always stand firm and be alert. If the enemy doesn't cease in trying to make our lives a living hell, we should have the same persistence to resist and continue pressing forward, trusting that God's plan is better than ours. The Bible assures us in James 4:7 that if we resist the devil, he will flee. What should we do while we stand firm? We praise Him, pray to Him, and wait on Him, until we receive our victory. To stand firm is a daily choice. And I personally choose to wholeheartedly trust in the One who has never failed me and has a perfect plan for my life. Things will unfold exactly the way He desires. And I believe the same can happen with you. The choice is *yours* to make!

Silent Reflection

God has a true sense of humor. It seems that at our lowest points in life, He uses us the most to affirm and encourage others who are at their lowest points. It seems unfair because they are receiving a good word when *you* need a good word. But just as God told Paul in 2 Corinthians 12:9, *"My grace is all you need. My power works best in weakness."* We too can receive the same grace for our challenges. Our weakness will become our strength through the power of Jesus Christ. When you encourage others, you are receiving courage yourself to confront and overcome your battles. For, it is a double-edged sword. If you give, you will receive, and it will become a win-win situation for everyone!

CHAPTER FOUR

trusted with trouble

We've all heard it said, "God has a sense of humor." Another common saying is, "If you want to make God laugh, tell Him your plans." And as frustrating as these sayings may be, His intentions with our lives will always be greater than ours. Despite my circumstances, I have had to learn that He is a good Father who loves me and has the very best set aside for me. It's hard to come to grips with this truth; but the only choice I've allowed myself to have is to simply believe in God's perfect and unique plan for my life.

My dad has always said that some people will have to fight a little more and a little harder than others. Well, both my parents have been a testament to that statement. Everything they have achieved in life and in ministry has not come easy. They have learned how to take all their fears and anxieties to the One who is able to help. I've admired their prayer warrior spirits, along with many other godly traits. So, it makes sense when my dad says that things don't always come easy. The question is: Will we give up?

The reason why I am so persistent in my faith, allowing myself no other option but to believe, is because I was raised in a household where there were no quitters. We pray, we believe, and we trust God's plans for our lives – no question about it! And I think that perseverance has allowed me to be disciplined in my faith. Notice I said *disciplined*, not *perfect*. I would be lying to you if I told you that I had faith every single day of my life, and that every season is a walk in the park. This is not true for me and it's not true for you. We all encounter times of doubt. And let's be honest! There are many moments when we want to quit; but it's the discipline that allows us to get up time after time and move forward.

I'm not a huge fan of running. I actually hate it! However, I've run my share of 5k's over the years, and have surprisingly enjoyed them. I haven't been the first one across the finish line, neither have I been the last. I always run these races with a couple of people, usually my sister and cousins. Amazingly, there comes a point in every race where you think you're going to give up. You either want to turn around and go home or finish the race walking. But this is why the people you run with become vitally important.

On several occasions, I remember wanting to give up in the middle of a race. I would hear my sister Kenia or one of my cousins, Miksi or Jasmin, cheer me on and encourage me to keep going. "Landy, don't give up, we are halfway there! You've got this!" Those were words of affirmation that gave me an energy boost to continue running my race at my pace. In life, we all have a race to run. And although everyone's race looks different and is run at different paces, the important thing to remember is to not give up. It's never easy, but it's worth it when we get to the finish line.

When we become persistent in our faith and in prayer, we become people who can be trusted by Almighty God. He rejoices when He finds someone who, despite the challenges at hand, remains on the solid ground of faith. You see, everyone has faith, and everyone can pray, but it is in those difficult moments when we're hit hard, when the kind of ground we are standing upon is revealed. Are we going to give up? Are we going to get mad at God because things are not going according to our plans? Or are we going to stick through the pain and continue to press forward? Only a few will do this because it's hard, and it takes courage when we're discouraged.

I want to tell you today that whether you are facing infertility challenges or any other troubles in life, God trusts you. The reason you are facing those things is because He can trust you with it. Yes, in those moments of solitude and despair, God trusts you. *"But I don't have strength, I just want to give up,"* you may say. Nevertheless, you have Someone on the sidelines cheering you on, saying, "You can do it!"

This reminds me of the story of Job. He was tested with trouble; and boy, did he go through some stuff! Every time I feel overwhelmed, I just think about Job and it makes me feel a little better. God trusted Job with trouble. The amplified version of Job 1:1 says that he was *"Blameless and upright, and one who feared God [with reverence] and abstained from and turned away from evil [because he honored God]."* Because Job was a man of integrity, God knew He could trust him with anything. He lost his family, his wealth, his health, and his friends, not because he did anything wrong, but because God was testing him. You see, our suffering is not always a result of some sin we've committed; sometimes God uses troubles to test us.

In Job 42:10, we read that the Lord restored the fortunes of Job when he prayed for his friends, giving him twice as much as he had before. Verse 12 says that the Lord blessed his latter days more than his beginning. In the story of Job, we see an example of faithfulness. No matter the situation, he stood steadfast. Yes, he was human and hurt like we all do. He had deep pain, both physically and emotionally. He wept, he mourned, and he even wished death upon himself; however, he never cursed God. He never abandoned the Lord. He was loyal. And this is the type of relationship God is seeking from you today – loyalty no matter what.

I love this quote from Priscilla Shirer from her book "God is Able." She says: *"We know what God can do, but we do not place our faith in what He can do, we place our faith in who He is."* God was able to trust Job with trouble because Job was faithful. Job never cursed Him once for all the disgrace he endured. Our loyalty should be to God alone, not in what He can do for us. When we place our faith in our God, we have the courage to say what Shadrach, Meshach, and Abednego said in their trial: *"I know God can do it, I know that He is able to save us from this fiery furnace. But if for some reason He does not do what I know He can, I will still worship Him because my praise goes far beyond what God can do."* What a powerful statement to say to the king right before being thrown into the furnace. Had these young men rejected God Almighty and bowed to King Nebuchadnezzar, their lives would have been spared from the fire; however, these brave young men valued loyalty much more, and were willing to risk their lives. Nothing would ever bring them to bend the knee to anyone else but God. And

I believe that the faith and the courage of these men revealed one of the greatest miracles recorded in the Bible.

I don't know what fiery furnace you may find yourself in. It might be infertility or something different. Regardless, we are *all* facing the intense heat of some fiery furnace. Some of our fires might be at level one, others at level four. You might find yourself at a level seven like the three Hebrew boys, incurring the wrath of the king who ordered that the furnace be turned up seven times hotter than normal. And yet, I'm here to give you hope! Just as God was present with these boys, and allowed nothing to happen to them, He is with *you*, sustaining you every moment. That is why you're still here.

If you're like me, you've thought, "Man, this situation should have taken me down. I don't know how I am still standing!" The answer is quite simple: God is in the furnace with you. And just as Shadrach, Meshach, and Abednego made it out alive without even the smell of fire on their clothes, you can too. If you put your trust in the One who can save you, He will see you through in such a way that you will appear poised, unscathed, and full of grace.

God is looking for people who He can trust when times get tough. It's easy to say, "God, I love and praise you" when all is well. But can you honestly say, "God, I will still worship you even if you don't heal me...Even if I don't ever have children...Even if I never get married... Even if you don't take this struggle away"? Can you truly say, "I will continue to be faithful and loyal to you"? These questions require honest answers.

Silent Reflection

God wants to restore everything you've lost. He wants to give you double for your trouble. But before He does that, He needs to know that you are trustworthy. Is God able to confidently say, "I can trust you, no matter what"? The truth is, many are not trustworthy, especially after going through troubles and trials. It's not easy being tested, because there's a lot of pressure that a person feels as he or she goes through the varied emotions in the test. However, it is vital to know that God is by your side, cheering you on, just like He did with Job. He has trusted you with this trouble and knows that although it may be hard, you will pass.

James 1:2-4 says, *"Consider it pure joy, my brothers and sisters, whenever you face trials of many kinds, because you know the testing of your faith produces perseverance. Let perseverance finish its work so that you may be mature and complete, not lacking anything."* Trials are not a sign of God's displeasure, but rather a divine instrument that brings perseverance into our lives. As crazy as it may sound, it's an honor to face difficulties because it means that God has trusted you with the troubles you are facing today. And if He trusts you with them, you will triumph over them.

CHAPTER FIVE

never easy

I've often asked myself this simple yet profound two-word question, "Why me?" I'm sure I'm not alone in this. At one point or another, you have certainly asked yourself that same question. I've seen throughout the years how for some, things come easily and for others, not so much. I'll be honest, I've struggled with this feeling for a long time. From the time I was in grade school I knew I needed to study harder to pass my math tests, as I've never been good at that subject. On the other hand, my husband Josh is a math whiz. This simple example demonstrates that there are things in life that come easy to some, while are difficult for others. As I got older, all my friends got married in their early twenties while I was still single. The same question was raised, "Why me?" Yes, friendships would spark but *the one* eluded me. I would get upset and say to myself, "It's never easy for me!"

I met my husband at thirty and got married at thirty-one. I thought my life was back on track, until we began trying to have a family. "Why me?" Those words began to creep up on me once again. I was no longer dealing with hypothetical math problems – I had a real-life problem! But much to my surprise, life is a lot like a math problem. With Algebra, there is always a solution to the problem; all you need to do is plug in the x and y. If you have the right formula, you will always have the right answer. Throughout these hard years of infertility, I have discovered that the problem will never be solved if you do not plug in the correct formula. And for me the formula has been my faith. Jesus has been my x and Christ has been my y. When I plug Jesus Christ into the problem, I will get an answer. Not my answer, not what I expect, not the results that I've been longing for, but the *right* answer. There have been times when I wanted to drop everything and give up. Let's be honest, your human nature can only take so much. But it is in those moments that I've been able to lean into God's Word and rest in His promises. He says in 2 Corinthians 12:9, *"My grace is sufficient for you, for my power is made perfect in weakness."*

No Test, No Testimony

Just recently, my perspective changed, and I began to ask myself this question: "Why *not* me?" Why must I feel this sense of entitlement as though I should be exempted from this test. Just like in school, you must take the test and pass it if you want to be promoted to the next grade. The same is true for us in the real world, as tests are necessary in order to show us what we are made of. Unfortunately, many believers have the misconception that because they are Christ-followers, they are exempt from trials and tribulations. However, Jesus says in John 16:33, *"These things I have spoken to you, that in Me you may have peace. In the world you will have tribulation;*

but be of good cheer, I have overcome the world." I especially love the phrase, "Be of good cheer," because it's telling us to have a positive outlook, to be encouraged, to "take heart" as another version states. Why? Because the solution has been given: *"I have overcome the world."* Jesus has overcome everything we could possibly deal with in life, whether sickness, financial crisis, family issues, or even our infertility struggles! He bore it all on the Cross.

When you can find joy amid your pain and smile through your tears, you're acing the test. It is important to remember that your test will be a reminder of God's faithfulness throughout your life. It will reveal the knowledge you have gained while studying and absorbing what the Teacher has taught you. God is our instructor and everyday there are lessons to be learned. The Word is our manual, the Book we go to for nourishment, growth, and knowledge, so that when the time comes to take the test, we can pass with flying colors.

You cannot testify about something you have not been through. Your test will become your testimony. Watch God turn your mess into a message because there are so many hurting people in the world going through exactly the same thing you have experienced, either currently or in the past, and they will need your encouragement to get them victoriously through their season. You see, there is nothing wasted in God's hands. Your season of struggle and pain is not wasted, as God will use it for your good, for the good of others, and for His glory.

Walking By

Although you may be walking through the darkest valley of your life, Psalm 23:4 serves as a reminder that you are simply walking by. This means that the dark valley you are in is temporary, because God is with you, which is why you shall fear no evil. Are you going to have dark days? Absolutely! You are human. However, you cannot and should not stay in that dark valley because it is not your place of residency. If you understand the difference between "walking by" and "moving in," you will not attempt to build a house in the valley! This is why the Bible says that you are "walking." And the word "walking" is an action verb. It means to move at a regular pace by lifting and setting down each foot in turn, never having both feet off the ground at once. It requires effort to lift and to move because with every step you take, you are moving further away from your pain and closer to a place of healing and restoration. God doesn't want you to stay at a standstill. He doesn't want you to wallow in your sorrows. His desire is to see you move forward in faith and for joy to be made evident in your life.

Silent Reflection

Yes, life is complicated and there are many challenges along the way, but there will always be a solution to our complicated problems. Just like we rely on a calculator to get the right answer, we need to rely on prayer, faith, and His Word to get us through those hard times. The road is never easy but it's so worth it when Jesus is by our side. Ask the Holy Spirit to change your perspective and help you see the beauty amid your ashes. There is a testimony to be told and the world must hear it from you. The test is not easy but in the name of Jesus, you will pass it.

CHAPTER SIX

*it is well
(is it really?)*

As I am writing this chapter, I am still childless. Months, even years have passed since I've really dedicated some time to writing. Honestly, I thought I would have had a child by now. And how wonderful would it be for my story to have a "happy ending"? That is the reason I have put this book off for so long, I've simply been waiting. But what happens when you wait and wait but nothing happens? What's the next step?

I've been waiting for the next move. Can you relate? Haven't you ever said, "If x, y, or z, doesn't happen, then I can't move forward"? As for me, the Lord began to tell me to *just write.* I replied, *"God, this is too painful. I don't want to write through my pain. I want my 'happily ever after' first."* Naturally, we would like for everything to be "fixed" and in its place before proceeding. And let's be honest! No one likes to wait, especially when you've been doing it for so long. It is much easier to put a Band-Aid over the pain, pretend everything is okay and just focus on other things. Everything seems fine until those raw emotions become exposed. The truth is that grief is real. It's a stormy ocean that hits you in waves. From one day to the next, you never know if you'll be battered by its emotional intensity.

It is in these moments that I've found myself drawing nearer to the Lord, even if I don't "feel" Him close by. I must remind myself that faith is not based on feelings, which change with the wind; but God's faith never wavers. This is why Paul reminds us in 2 Corinthians 5:7 that we walk by faith and not by sight. If we were to be led by what we see, it would be impossible to believe God for the impossible, as reason and logic would replace faith. The Bible also says in Hebrews 11:6 that without faith it is impossible to please God. So, when we put our faith and trust in God, we are saying that despite what our natural eyes see, we choose to believe His report. Although I won't disregard the emotions I am feeling in the moment, I will not allow them to control me because my faith is in the Lord.

Friends, it is okay to cry, scream, and even become angry. It is okay to be confused and even to grieve. I'll take it a step further! It is *necessary* to do so. What is not okay is to stay in that place and allow yourself to be manipulated by emotions. God loves you too much to let you go through this process alone. He hurts with you. But He does not want you to stay hurt! 1 Peter 5:7 says, *"Casting all your cares on Him, because He cares about you."* I don't know about you but there's something about that verse that brings me so much peace. And throughout Scripture we see how God's care for His children is evident. We see this in Psalm 55:22 when

David exclaims, *"Give your burdens to the Lord and He will take care of you. He will not permit the godly to slip and fall."* It is encouraging to know that we can give all our worries to the Lord, the one person who has the solution to our problem. At times, it is okay to share your problems with friends; but while they can be present for you, they are not generally able to solve those problems. But how awesome is it that the One who can resolve our troubles and put our souls to rest, is the One who is telling us to give our burdens to Him?

Our Heavenly Father longs to take care of us in every possible way, even more than our earthly fathers. We know that a responsible father is one who takes the burden of the household and assures his family members that everything will be alright. As our heavenly Father, God does not want us to worry about the things we cannot handle, rather to focus on Him as Jehovah Jireh – our provider. He will provide, sustain, and meet all our needs, whether they are emotional, mental, physical, or spiritual. His care gives us a level of responsibility to simply invite Him into our lives. He wants to be included in all our plans. He rejoices when we make Him a priority in our lives. Even right now, you might feel as though your life doesn't make sense, your heart is broken, dreams are shattered, and you don't know how to recover from the agonizing pain that constantly tortures you. Even in this moment when you might believe God to be distant, as though He hasn't been there for you, He is present! For, when He seems the furthest away, He is nearer than you know.

His Eyes Cried

What I love about Jesus is that he is so relatable and can identify with pain. In John 11:35, the shortest verse in the Bible, we read that "Jesus wept." That the Son of God, in all His divinity, was able to hurt when others hurt, is incredible. His precious and perfect eyes leaked tears of sorrow alongside His friends. You see, Jesus had a friend named Lazarus who was very dear to Him. The Bible says that Lazarus was sick. His sisters, Martha and Mary, who were also friends of Jesus, sent Him a message about their sick brother. Now, you would think that Jesus would have dropped everything to be by His friend's side; after all, that's what friends are for, right? Instead, He decided not to show up when everyone else expected Him. Think about that for a second! How many times have you wanted something so bad that you've begged for it? Think back to your childhood, and recall saying something like, "Mom, can you get me this? Please?!" It is true that in every stage of our lives, we've wanted things "right now!" But Jesus, in the case of His friends' request for Him to come, knew that He couldn't – not in the timing they wanted.

Please understand, as I type these words, I am preaching to myself. Please know that God is not withholding anything from you, He is simply cooking up something bigger and better for you, and for me. Isaiah 55:8-9 says, *"For my thoughts are not your thoughts, neither are your ways my ways," declares the Lord. "As the heavens are higher than the earth, so are my ways higher than your ways and my thoughts than your thoughts."* His thought process is different than ours. Honestly, if we were to think just like God, wouldn't that diminish who He is? In the case of Lazarus, Jesus showed up four days too late, as Lazarus had already died and was laid in a tomb. When Jesus arrived, His eyes became full of tears. He mourned the loss of His friend alongside his sisters and everyone who was there. Martha and Mary were upset, however, as He wasn't there when they needed Him the most. I can imagine Lazarus wondering where Jesus was, expecting Him to be by his side. They had shared so many special moments together. He had heard so many great testimonies of his friend healing the sick. Surely, Jesus would heal him too, right? But Lazarus died without seeing his friend or receiving a healing. Yet, despite what others may have thought, Jesus had a plan to fulfill, which was to bring glory to God.

Sometimes, God won't act when we want Him to. In His sovereignty, He will allow us to experience pain, not because He wants us to hurt, but because there is a bigger plan. Although we may weep, we will not be alone, because He will weep right beside us. And when we mourn, He will mourn with us. As lonely as we may feel during the grieving process, He is with us grieving. What I love about Jesus is that He *"Works for the good of those who love Him, who have been called according to His purpose"* (Romans 8:28), and therefore knows that the pain is only temporary. David says in Psalm 30:5 that *"Weeping may endure for a night, but joy comes in the morning."* In the case of Lazarus, Jesus knew that joy was about to make its grand appearance in the lives of Martha and Mary, as they would no longer mourn but were about to celebrate the triumphant return of their brother from the dead.

Why would Jesus even bother to cry and be saddened by the passing of His friend, if He knew what was about to happen? He knew Lazarus would come back to life, so why even bother with tears? The simple answer is that

He cared. In this passage and throughout Scripture we see that Jesus had deep compassion for those who were suffering. This gives us a glimpse of how sympathetic Jesus is toward our afflictions. I repeat, He doesn't want us to hurt nor does He rejoice in our afflictions. Lamentations 3:33 is clear when it says, *"For He does not willingly bring affliction or grief to anyone."* Jesus is more interested in doing the will of the Father to bring Him glory.

I've often thought, "Couldn't God just avoid it all?" It would have been easier for us both. He could have easily just written off the suffering in His divine playbook. Life would be less chaotic had my pain not happened, had God just answered my prayers, had He given me a child. And I know you have probably asked the same question. And although He certainly has the power to keep us from things, He chooses differently. He allows us to walk through it so that He can get all the glory. He could have stopped it, but He didn't, because a greater reward awaits us. It may be four days away, a few months away, or even several years away. However long it takes, God is with you every step of the way, all the while setting you up for your biggest comeback. As broken as you are right now, God is preparing something special for you that will ultimately bring Him all the glory.

Beautifully Broken

Psalm 34:18 declares that *"The Lord is close to the brokenhearted and saves those who are crushed in spirit."* As hard it may be to understand this, God is closest when we're in pain. Maybe you're reading these pages and cannot relate to infertility or to a miscarriage, but you can certainly relate to pain, disappointment, shame, guilt, or hardship. You can identify some point where you have been hurt, your heart has been broken, or perhaps shattered beyond repair. If you have felt alone, or misunderstood, then Psalm 34 is for you.

God has been near and has helped you get through it. Just think about it! You're still here by the grace of God. When you say, *"I don't know how I made it, but I did,"* know that it was *God.* Perhaps you've uttered the words, *"I am not supposed to be alive,"* but you've seen another day, another year; it was God who saved you. I will remind you of a wonderful promise in Deuteronomy 31:6, that I constantly remind myself of: *"Be strong and courageous. Do not be afraid or terrified because of them, for the Lord your God goes with you; He will never leave your nor forsake you."* What is it that is terrifying you today? Is it infertility? Is it the fear of never becoming a mom? Is it not being able to find "Mr. Right"? Or might it be a diagnosis of some sickness? Whatever is troubling your heart, surrender it to the One who has promised to never leave or forsake you. He's telling you today, "We are walking through this together because I am not going anywhere!" Will you give Him the broken pieces of your heart? Even if it's shattered beyond repair, I know that He can make something beautiful out of your broken pieces. You may be broken but He still sees beauty, that you're beautifully broken.

Silent Reflection

You must believe that God is in control regardless of the circumstances, when things are good, or things are bad, whether you are sad or happy. The key is to keep moving forward. Maybe your story is different than mine; but we all have a story. We all know pain, we all hurt. You may be in a season of joy and happiness. If so, we celebrate you today. Just remember to lift those around you who are not sharing that same season. Perhaps your season looks like mine. If so, I want your greatest takeaway from this book to be that *you are not alone*! You do not have to fight your battles solo. God is with you! And if you can identify with *Silent Cries*, I want you to begin opening up and talking to people who can help you get through this season of sorrow.

CHAPTER SEVEN

way maker

After countless procedures, surgeries, treatments, and medications, we decided to re-visit in vitro fertilization (IVF), again. We began the second round of IVF because according to my doctors, this would be my best chance of getting pregnant. With a different doctor in a different facility, I was very hopeful. This time it would be different, I just knew it. We prayerfully considered it and felt peace with the decision to proceed. We were going to act in faith and believe God for a financial miracle as this was our second time around, and it would be very costly.

Have you ever been so "sure" of a decision you've made, only to ask yourself later, "What did I just do?" Well, that was me. The timing seemed perfect, and the season was appropriate. What's more, my husband and I had seen glimpses of God's hand all over this opportunity. One of those times occurred just as we were getting ready to go to IVF orientation. Minutes before class began, we received a phone call regarding the cost of medication.

After being told that I would have to order and pay for it that week, I realized that we could not afford it. What was worse, we were required to pay the full amount out-of-pocket. I was heartbroken and cried my eyes out.

I showed up to the class ready to tell the doctors of our defeat, when out of nowhere, God's provision arrived! To us, it was proof that God was in this, and that He would grant us our long-awaited baby. We even had a theme song throughout this crucial season, called "Way Maker." The chorus says, *"Way Maker, miracle worker, promise keeper, light in the darkness. My God, that is who You are."* We were witnessing right before our eyes the miracle He was working in our lives. He promised us children and to us, this was the vehicle He would use to bring that promise to pass. Finally, we would see the light at the end of our dark season, a light that would shine so bright and bring so much joy and happiness to our family.

I had never been so sure about something like I was about this round of IVF. I could finally breathe, as my dream of fertility was about to take shape. I had one of the best doctors in the state of Florida treating me with a success rate in the top 90 percentile. I was willing to endure the discomfort of many doctor visits, injections, bloodwork, and other various procedures, knowing I would soon be pregnant. Certainly, God had seen my faithfulness over all the years of delay and would now reward me with motherhood.

It is so funny how we think we have God all figured out! Well, if I'm being honest, it's actually *aggravating*! I mean, just when I think I understand God's plans, life seems to crumble in front of me. The truth is, nine out of ten times, I attribute *my* plan as being *His* plan. This type of scenario has led me to anger, tears, and fights, many times. But all of it leads me right back to the feet of Jesus, again and again, where I surrender my ideas to Him.

I began round two of IVF in August 2018. Five days before Christmas I finally got the long-awaited phone call. God heard our prayers and we were *finally* pregnant! As I heard the news over the phone, making the nurse repeat it over and over again, I was shaking with nerves. I was pregnant! After eight years of marriage, God made a way for us to experience the miracle of life. This was certainly a Christmas miracle, that reminded me of our theme song: *"Way Maker, miracle worker, promise keeper, light in the darkness. My God, that is who You are."*

The joy of this epic moment was short-lived, however, when we lost our child a few weeks later. It was the most devastating moment of my entire life. I was lost and empty, like I had no soul left. It felt like a cruel joke. I tried so hard not to get mad at God, but I just couldn't withhold my fury. It simply was not fair! Why allow me to go through all the physical, mental, and emotional pain if in the end, it wasn't going to work out? Why not spare me from the multiple daily injections and weekly doctor visits? Why allow me to go through the egg retrieval and the embryo transfer process, which I endured under general anesthesia? I recall vividly the doctors and nurses shaking their heads over my case, because out of twenty-eight egg retrievals and fourteen embryos, there was only *one* match, which was implanted perfectly. And here I now stood, after a few weeks, the doctors telling me that my baby wouldn't make it. I needed another miracle, and this time it was for the child inside my womb.

A few days before my miscarriage, I preached at my home church, saying goodbye to 2018 and welcoming 2019. It was a great night where I was full of faith, preaching and believing once again for my miracle. The title of my message was, "Sweet Dreams." A few days later, I went to the doctor to hear the baby's heartbeat; however, they couldn't even see the sac nor hear a heartbeat. I was crushed and felt as though my heart stopped beating. Little did I know I would be saying "sweet dreams" to my sweet baby a week and a half later.

I mourned my miscarriage; I mourned the loss of my child. I didn't want to tell the entire world what was going on, only a few close friends and family who helped me get through this difficult period. A few months later, I felt a tug in my heart that I needed to share my story. And so, I decided to open up on my personal blog. On the day of my birthday, I became vulnerable in sharing my experience. Here is what I wrote:

"Today is my birthday, and I am celebrating a huge milestone in my life. But this year's celebration looks quite different than those in the past. A couple months ago, I envisioned a huge gathering with friends and family where I would share the biggest news ever. But a lot has happened since then. This year's different. There will be no celebration, there will be no party, and there will be no grand announcement. This time it's different.

"I've been struggling to share this for a few months – like really, really struggling. But I just feel like God is pushing me to speak. And I will admit, sometimes it sucks to be transparent and vulnerable, because you become exposed. For the most part, I am a very private person; but there's an area of my life in which I must be vocal for the sake of anyone out there who may be going through the same thing. This requires me getting out of my comfort zone and sacrificing my privacy for your sake, or for someone you know.

"For those who know my story, I've been struggling with infertility for about eight years, and have publicly opened up about it last year. After many attempts to get pregnant, along with surgeries, treatments, medicines, and IVF, nothing has worked until late last year. Our dream came true and we were able to get pregnant. We were so excited to finally become parents! Even though still in the womb, our baby celebrated so much with us. Baby was also present when mama preached on New Year's Eve. It was magical. I remember God giving me that message which I titled: "Sweet Dreams." Little did I know that twelve days later, I would be telling my baby Sweet Dreams…forever.

"My precious angel went to be with the Lord in January. This angel was my child, making me a mother for the very first time, after eight agonizing years. My baby was a miracle, proving that in fact, I could get pregnant. Despite the pain and grief that is still so tangibly present, I still cling on to hope and continue to believe for the future. And I can't wait to meet my sweet angel one day.

"Why am I sharing this? Because miscarriage is so raw and so real. I never thought infertility would be added to my life's resume. And when it happened, it was shocking and numbing all at once. For many weeks, I was numb to my surroundings. I had to quickly delete the baby apps, unsubscribe from the baby email listings, and stop taking my weekly baby-bump pictures. I had to close that painful chapter in my life. Everything stopped as my hopes and dreams shattered right before my eyes. Grief is painful. I can now say, I know how it feels to lose a child. Its heart-wrenching. How do you move forward?

"I've had to learn how to deal with grief and navigate through my feelings. I am thankful for my support system, for my husband and my family, as well as special friends who have walked with me on this painful road. I am thankful for my Heavenly Father. I've found refuge in prayer and God's Word which has helped me silence the voice of the enemy whenever he whispers lies in my ear. I am also thankful for a book by Lysa Terkeurst, that has helped me process my disappointment, called: *It's Not Supposed to Be This Way: Finding Unexpected Strength When Disappointments Leave You Shattered.* I began reading it two weeks after my loss.

"One thing that Lysa Terkeurst says is, *"If the enemy can isolate us, he can influence us."* You see, there are so many women who are shattered beyond belief and their pain is keeping them from receiving help, like a word of hope. So many couples are dealing with infertility by themselves, and so many women grieving the loss of their babies are either too afraid or too ashamed to share their stories. I want to tell you that you don't have to walk this painful and lonely road by yourself. There are people that God will place in your path who will help you if you allow them to do so. And if I can encourage you with something from my journey, I would say this: There is *nothing* to be ashamed of. You are normal. You are fearfully and wonderfully made. God does not make mistakes. He is not done with you. He is still writing your story. A new sentence begins after a period. A new chapter begins when you flip the page. Yesterday, I received this quote by Steven Furtick, from my cousin: *"If He is the Alpha and Omega, and He wrote your beginning and your end, your A to Z, shouldn't you trust Him with everything in-between?"*

"As I am writing this, I feel deep sorrow because like I said, this was going to be a magical, birthday weekend. As a masterful planner, I had it all worked out. I would have been well into my second trimester, halfway past the middle mark. I would have loved to reveal the gender of my baby this weekend during my birthday celebration.

Instead, my big reveal is to let you know that I have an angel in heaven that is celebrating my birthday with me. This is not the type of celebration I expected – it's different.

"I don't know why things happen the way they do. God is sovereign, however, and if I knew all the answers, He would not be God. I am still processing this loss, as I have good days and not so good days. Saturdays are particularly tough because it was the day I would faithfully take my bump pictures.

"One thing that I've learned with grief is that you can't suppress your feelings, you can't hide, and you can't attempt to skip the process. If you want to heal, you must allow yourself to feel the hurt. You must go through the process of pain in order to heal. Lysa Terkeurst writes, *"To deny my feelings any voice is to rob me of being human, but to let my feelings be the only voice will rob my soul of healing perspectives with which God wants to comfort me and carry me forward."*

"Our feelings and our faith will conflict with each other, but we cannot stay planted in our feelings, as our dwelling place must be in faith. Today, my birthday may seem different, my celebration may be quieter than usual, but I can stubbornly say, "I still believe!" My life is anchored in faith by the Author and Finisher of all things. Jesus is my hope and I will not be shaken. I am constantly reminded of this unshakable life I've been given by a picture on my office wall that says, "Promise Still Stands." I know that I serve a God of miracles. And I am here believing not only for myself but for you, your sister, your aunt, your friend, or your co-worker, for their miracle as well. There is nothing impossible for Him. Although your situation may look different than mine, you can still trust that God has a firm grip on you, on your family, on your finances, on your health, and on everything else that you need. Your pain is not wasted, as He will use your story for His glory.

"You must serve only the Lord your God. If you do, I will bless you with food and water and I will protect you from illness. There will be no miscarriages or infertility in your land, and I will give you long, full lives" (Exodus 23:25-26).

"Be Encouraged, Be Blessed!" (Blog posted on March 28, 2019)

Silent Reflection

As the song goes, *"You are here, moving in our midst, I worship You, I worship You. You are here, working in this place, I worship You, I worship You."* As I am typing this on my laptop, a few days after my due date of August 2019, I've come to realize that all I can do is worship. God is still here, moving and working on my behalf. Grief is difficult and it comes in waves, but the one constant thing that remains is my worship. While He heals my broken heart, I will praise Him. While He continues to work a miracle in my life, I will continue to worship Him.

While you wait for God to make a way in your situation, worship Him. Even if you don't understand what He is allowing, trust Him because He is at work. Regardless of your circumstance, He is the *"Way maker, miracle worker, promise keeper, light in the darkness. My God, that is who You are."*

CHAPTER EIGHT

promise still stands

I have three white picture frames that hang above my office's black couch, that say, "Promise Still Stands." This is a daily reminder that I have a choice to either believe in God's promises for me or give up. It seems like a simple choice, however, every day I must be intentional with this decision. Some days it is a no-brainer, as I know that God has me covered. Other days, He just feels so distant that I don't even know if it's worth it anymore. Sometimes, it feels like I am wasting my time praying, believing, trusting, writing, and quoting Scriptures, as time keeps passing by. And if there is one thing you don't regain, it's time! I cannot simply hit "rewind" and return to my twenties or even thirties.

You see, the reason I am being raw in this book is because I understand that life can be a rollercoaster ride of emotions. After a while, you have absolutely nothing left to give, not even to God. But what I love about Him is that He knows us so well; there's no sense in masking our feelings. He wants us to be real, just like I'm being real with you right now. Sometimes, you don't want to keep believing that the "Promise Still Stands," because it's so far from your reality; it feels safer not to continually get your hopes up. And whereas it's okay to feel this way, what do you do next?

Friend, there comes a point in life when you must be intentional with your decisions. We all have the daily choice to either surrender to God's perfect will and His perfect timing, or to distrust Him. To *surrender* means "to cease resistance." It means "to give in, to accept, to yield, to submit." I know what you might be thinking! I just said an ugly word – *submit*. This is a word that gives a lot of us trouble. You see, if we are ever going to get to a place of peace, joy, and contentment in life, we must submit to God's will for our lives, even if things don't turn out how we envisioned them, or in the time we expected.

The Bible calls Jesus the "Author and Finisher of our faith." Therefore, we must fix our eyes on Him. However, we often find ourselves too busy fixing our eyes on our issues, on our bodies, on what the doctors are saying, or on what the diagnoses could possibly mean. And although it's good to stay informed and be proactive, we must shift our vision from the problem to the Problem Solver. What if I told you, I knew a doctor who had a perfect track record of healing sicknesses and helping women have babies? What if his practice was located in your city and people from all over the world traveled to see him? What if I told you there were countless women who wished they had the opportunity to be seen by him? What if you knew that many people would do anything to make that trip possible? What if I told you that this doctor knows you by name and has opened a slot just for you?

You didn't have to ask for an appointment, it was just given to you! Moreover, the cost is covered! You wouldn't have to worry about insurance covering it, or what your out-of-pocket cost would be – it's paid in full! And what if I told you this doctor's name is *Jesus*?! Friends, you can fix your eyes on Him, as He is the solution to your every problem, and will meet you right where you are.

"I hear you Landy, but why hasn't Jesus healed me?" you might ask. The truth is, I don't know. What I *do* know is that He is our healer. I love how Isaiah 53:5 is translated in the Amplified Version: *"But He was wounded for our transgressions, He was crushed for our wickedness [our sin, our injustice, our wrongdoing]; The punishment [required] for our well-being fell on Him, and by His stripes (wounds) we are healed."* We are healed in the name of Jesus, and we are made whole in Him. Just remember that sometimes our healing will look different than what we expected. It may come as a physical healing, but also as a spiritual or emotional restoration.

I also know that if you fix your eyes on Him, just as Peter did for a brief moment in Matthew 14, you will be able to walk on water, no matter the intensity of the storms that arise. You may be feeling scared, but if you focus on Jesus rather than the storm, He will guide you to safety. Hebrew 6:19 reminds us that our hope in Jesus is an anchor for the soul, sure and steadfast. And just as an anchor secures a boat in place so it won't drift off, our hope in Jesus Christ keeps us immovable.

I am not saying that putting our hope in Jesus makes everything easy. No way! I still have my rough days. I'm still grieving. I still have questions. However, I choose to stand on His promises. As I said earlier, standing is a choice. Why am I still standing? Because I have made the decision to stand on His promises, regardless if it makes me look stubborn – I know He will fulfill them! As the Scriptures say, He is not a liar and does not go back on His word. Would I have wanted my life to look different? Absolutely! But when you make a conscious decision to surrender to your Maker's will, you can come to terms with what life looks like right now. And although it might look different, I continue to trust that He is guiding me in the right direction, and I will not sink despite the hurricanes that rage along the way. He is my anchor and I will trust Him. When all else has failed, it is His Word that has sustained me without fail.

I connect with Elevation Worship's song, "Do It Again" because it says:

"I've seen You move, come move these mountains
And I believe, I'll see You do it again
You made a way, where there was no way
And I believe, I'll see you do it again"
"Your promise still stands
Great is Your faithfulness, faithfulness
I'm still in Your hands
This is my confidence, You've never failed me yet"

The reason we can firmly say, "God, I'll see you do it again," is not because of arrogance or naiveté; we are bold in this declaration because we trust Him. If we will remember what He's done for us in the past, our outlook towards the future will become more hopeful. And this becomes a pivotal moment when our mindset shifts from one of complaints to that of praise. God will do it again! It may not be the way He did it last time, or the way in which you expect, but He will do something, and it will be great! It is a daily choice to believe that God will fulfill His promises to us, regardless of how we feel from one day to the next. Just keep reminding yourself that God's Word is constant, and He can be trusted!

Silent Reflection

Maybe your life feels like a yo-yo right now. You're up one day and down the next. You believe today and doubt tomorrow. However, I want to encourage you to doubt your doubts! Stop doubting what God can do and start believing that all things are possible. In John 11:40, Jesus says, *"Did I not tell you that if you believed you would see the glory of God?"* The only way you will see the glory of God in your life is if you doubt your doubts and feed your faith. The choice is yours…what will you choose?

CHAPTER NINE

*circle around
your circle*

Hardships are processes that have a way of shutting you down and shutting you up. They tend to produce this kind of pattern: initial shock, followed by crying, screaming, getting angry, causing you to finally withdraw. It's as though your hardship takes complete control of your mind and emotions to the point that you feel obligated to shut up. For me, it took a few years to open my mouth and begin talking about my infertility. I was dying on the inside, screaming words that weren't able to leave my mouth. Although everything seemed normal on the outside, I was deteriorating on the inside.

I'm here to say that this is *not* okay. In fact, it is now time to find your voice! If you need to cry, then cry. If you need to scream, then scream. If you are angry, have questions, or need to vent, be angry, ask your questions, and vent! Just do so within healthy boundaries. And know that you cannot continue to suppress your feelings. We are allowed to feel these emotions, as this is what makes us human beings and not robots.

Although it has become cliché, I want you to know that you are not alone. You don't have to walk this journey by yourself. Whether you're facing infertility or a different challenge, there are women all over the world going through exactly the same thing. And maybe, just maybe, if you're courageous enough to find your voice in the midst of the pain, disappointment, and heartache, you can offer hope to someone out there who seems hopeless. Just remember to surround yourself with other women who will encourage you, not pull you down.

Another piece of advice to consider, is finding an inner circle where you can fit in. You might be asking, "What do you mean by 'inner circle'?" Well, after looking up several definitions for "inner circle," I found this one from Collins Dictionary: "a small group of people within a larger group who have a lot of power, influence, or special information." Okay, that sounds especially important, right? It basically means, find a small group of people with whom you can trust and be yourself. You should feel comfortable enough to expose your vulnerabilities, something that your larger circle of acquaintances don't necessarily get to see. Your inner circle should be a judgment-free zone.

Many of us already have a few friends who can be trusted with our confidence – start there. Keep in mind, it's important to *circle around your circle*, because not everyone belongs in your group. Not everyone has the right intentions, not everyone is patient and understanding of your process. And it's of utmost importance to be around people who can journey with you in a healthy way. Your circle should be full of people who can say, "We are in this together no matter what." This is a circle who will see you pull through, cheer you on, and be strong when you're weak. This is what I mean by "circle around your circle."

Walls Come Down

It takes a real friend to know a real friend, one who can decipher the sadness behind the smile. Therefore, it is vital to check up on your friends, because you never know what pain they may be masking. This requires us to be intentional with the people in our circle. Knowing who your friends are, you should therefore be able to perceive when something is off. Above all, prayer is key. We pray for wisdom and discernment, which are crucial allies in our attempt to navigate through our friends' feelings. The hope is that we will help them peel back the self-imposed layers that work as a defense mechanism. I know from personal experience, that this process is difficult, as it is much easier to pretend everything is okay rather than be open to get at the root. It's a lot simpler to fake the funk, put on a smile, stay busy, and act like everything is normal. It seems justifiable to pretend, especially so that you don't get those looks of pity from everyone around.

Now, inner-circle friends don't throw pity parties for the friend they are attempting to help. Trust me, that is the *last* thing she wants! It's embarrassing, awkward, and uncomfortable; and by doing that, you're just pushing her away. So, don't do that. Recognize the pain but offer healthy alternatives for her to get her mind off the problem. Invite her out to do something fun, help build her faith by encouraging her with the Word of God, or just pray with her. Be present and be consistent. Don't forget about her just because a few weeks have passed, or because you assume "she's fine"; remember, this is a daily struggle for her. And I promise you that if you are genuine and sincerely care about her, the walls she has built will come down. It takes time. When we are persistent in a loving way, our friend will open up, and everything she has been suppressing will begin to spill like a fountain. And that, my inner-circle friend, is how you achieve vulnerability from a walled-off woman.

Be the One

I am so thankful for the people God has placed in my path for this specific season I'm currently experiencing. Although they cannot relate to infertility or miscarriage, my family has been my constant, as their love and support has been crucial. However, there is just something about surrounding yourself with people who have walked in your shoes and "get you." I am extremely grateful for friends who have helped me along my journey, friends who have walked this path before and were able to help me navigate through the gut-wrenching loss of my baby.

You see, relatability is important. If you're struggling with something, find someone that you can reach out to, someone who has gone through a similar situation. It will require you to put yourself out there. Keep in mind, it may not happen right away. But when you finally connect with the right person, you'll see how refreshing it will be for your soul. To know that someone out there knows exactly how you feel is a game changer. It's even more rewarding and hope-inducing when you know that they've been able to overcome their challenges.

If you're that person who has overcome a particular struggle and you're "on the other side," be the one who goes out and finds someone with whom you can share your experience. Trust me, all you need to say is, "I was in the exact place you are now. I know it's hard, and I know it hurts, but you will overcome this. Look at me! I was able to do it, you can too." These words are a ray of sunshine that brightens up even the darkest hole someone may find themselves in. Don't underestimate yourself. Your story is powerful, no matter how small it might seem. If you were able to survive it, others can too. It all starts with one person, like yourself, who is brave enough to share her testimony with another person. If that person does the same thing, and this continues, before long many people will be helped and healed. There is strength in numbers, *and* there is power in one.

Silent Reflection

We live in a world where people are silently screaming for help, just wanting to be heard. But it's hard to vocalize deep-rooted pain. Ask the Lord to give you the wisdom to discern when your friends are not okay. Ask Him how you can show up for them. Your friends need you, the loving and compassionate *you*, the one who will be patient with them and will cry with them, even if they don't express the reason behind their tears. Be the one to circle around them without giving up on them. And if you're the friend in need of help, trust that God will place people on your path who will journey this process with you. Don't be afraid to reach out to people who've had similar experiences, as nine out of ten times, they will be delighted to help you along the way. Never believe the ugly lie of the enemy that we can do life alone – we *need* each other. It's just not possible to live outside of community. And when we begin to shift our mentality from *me* to *we*, the positive impact we make on society will be evident to all. Your friends need you and you need your friends. Circle around your circle!

CHAPTER TEN

fertility faith

(by Sabrina, Mileidy, & Rosa)

Sabrina's Words

My experience with the trauma of infertility was one I thought I had healed from, until I would be reminded of being barren. Whenever I would hear the words "barren" out loud, it would take the wind out of me. You see, I got married at the age of 20, an age that created high expectations that I would have children early on. After some time passed, however, I slowly submerged into the waters of doubt, questioning whether I had what it took to be a mother. This was compounded by the fact that becoming pregnant became a seemingly insurmountable task.

Coming from a pastoral family, heavily rooted in my faith, I brought this situation to God, because my fears of incompetency and thoughts of the unknown world of maternity overcame me. Then I read Genesis 20:17-18 and became reassured:

"Then Abraham prayed to God and God healed Abimelech, his wife, and his maidservants, and they started having babies again. For God had shut down every womb in Abimelech's household on account of Sarah, Abraham's wife."

This truth set me free! By His sovereignty, God opens and shuts wombs. Therefore, I had no reason to be fearful as to whether I should have kids. God reassured me that *He* is the giver of life. More than a decade went by and the doubts, fears, along with that divine reassurance turned into complacency. I thought to myself, "Becoming a mother is not for me…I can live with that." It was during this time that my first marriage fell apart, and the possibility of becoming a mother was now out of the picture. I thought I came to terms with it until one day, in one of the darkest moments of my barren season, I had a vision.

I was resting on my bed and saw the brightness of a lightning strike. It was so close and so bright that it startled me. But before I was overcome with fear, I looked to my right and there was a beautiful baby boy, full of light, right next to me. Fear turned to extreme excitement as I began to admire this baby. Just as I was getting familiar with him, there was another lighting strike. This time, the bright strike was on my left. As I turned, I couldn't believe my eyes – it was another beautiful boy! When the vision ended, I was not happy, and I began to question God. I said: "If what I saw is of you, Lord, why would you choose the most barren season of my life to show me it? Why would you show me something like that?" I felt his response deep in my heart, as if I could hear his loving, fatherly voice saying: "I give dreams to the brokenhearted. I give dreams to the most incapable people. In the end, I get the glory."

Years later, I found love again and remarried. And in this time, I found myself holding my first streak of "lighting" – my first-born son who we named "AJ." It was a quick meeting between him and I, because just a few minutes out of the womb, we became aware that something was terribly wrong…he wasn't breathing! More bad news followed. He was placed on a ventilator, having an enlarged heart, an infection in his blood, liver issues, and deafness. It was a terrorist attack on my faith. None of these maladies coincided with the beautiful pregnancy including the many health exams I had during that period. My husband and I and the rest of our family surrounded ourselves with praying people from around the world, and together, we began declaring life over AJ. We battled fear, doubt, and hopelessness every day. Things did not look good. That was until…God! He began a complete healing in AJ's body, which we are still witnessing today, like a progressive miracle as he thrives despite some of the remaining limitations and challenges.

Three years later, as I was just getting the hang of being a mom, fitting into the role I once feared, a *big* surprise appeared. This surprise was just as big as the one on that dark day when God gave me a vision of two lightning strikes. We had another baby boy, named "Lucas." I passionately believe that God still gives dreams to the incapable. He trusts dreams in the hands of those who don't appear to be qualified.

Sabrina Yudith

Sabrina Yudith and her husband Aggeo serve as Associate Pastors at Iglesia de Dios Casa de Refugio in

Miami Gardens, Florida. She is also a worship leader and a recording artist.

Mileidy's Words

There is a hidden truth and heartbreak when having a miscarriage after healthy pregnancies. I experienced this firsthand. Suffering two miscarriages after already having kids came as a shock, which made moving forward extremely difficult. You see, my husband Donni and I are high school sweethearts and have loved each other our entire lives. We began building our family late 2013. We had two easy, healthy pregnancies. Our daughter Milanni was born in August 2014 and we welcomed our son Jethri in January 2016. When I saw two pink lines on my third pregnancy test, I was filled with joy, excitement, and an abundance of nervousness for what life would be like with three little ones. I made my first prenatal appointment and calculated my due date online, as I had done in past pregnancies. But the one thought that never crossed my mind was that we would never make it to that date.

Sixteen weeks later, accompanied by my husband Donni, I miscarried at home. Just as with full-term births, it was a physically taxing time with the typical full-term contractions. I later developed signs of infection and learned that remnants of the placenta were still intact, requiring a dilation and curettage. I was still nursing my son Jethri at the time. The general anesthesia required due to the D & C caused an instant impact on my milk supply and I was unable to continue nursing. My healing following this ordeal was physically, mentally, and spiritually painful.

In September of 2017, God, in his infinite mercy, blessed us with our rainbow baby, Malakai. He brought redemption, joy, and so much happiness to our family, so much so that I still struggle putting it into words.

Following Malakai's birth, we became pregnant with our fifth – a beautiful baby with a beating heart. Despite having a healthy pregnancy, however, our numerous plans ended in a very unexpected miscarriage. This second miscarriage turned my world upside down. I began having panic and anxiety attacks almost daily. I was later diagnosed with post-traumatic stress disorder. These are just some of the many things I didn't expect when I was no longer expecting.

During my miscarriages, I found it extremely hard to know what, if anything, to tell my kids. I found it difficult to answer their questions while I was under distress. The trauma of having to go home and tell my children that our babies hadn't survived was one of the hardest things I've ever had to do. I found immense comfort hugging the children I already had, but it was difficult parenting my rambunctious toddlers in the fog of postpartum life without a baby. Both times, my hormones went wild, extra weight stuck around, and my children asked me often why my baby died.

I found that having other children after a miscarriage was both a blessing and a burden. I struggled finding time to grieve the babies we lost while managing the demands of our other living children. If this wasn't enough to fill me with guilt, I discovered that many loved ones were not empathetic of the losses, because we already had other kids. Our loss was often diminished by people saying insensitive things like, "You already have three beautiful children," or "It wasn't meant to be." This marginalized my grief over the loss of the babies we were planning to add to our family. All of this led me to join a support group and begin therapy. I realized I wasn't alone in how I felt, and that we truly are better together. And although our family has always been fueled by faith, love, and perseverance, we added numerous therapy sessions to that list.

After all this trauma, we were blessed with another rainbow baby in October 2019. I was reminded of Isaiah 61:3 where God says, *"To all who mourn, He will give a crown of beauty for ashes, a joyous blessing instead of mourning, festive praise instead of despair. In their righteousness, they will be like great oaks that the LORD has planted for His own glory."*

But for us to be made beautiful, we must give Him our ashes. We must offer our mourning fully to Him to experience the joy only He can provide. As a miscarriage and rainbow mom, I've learned that although God meets us right where we are, He doesn't leave us there.

With love,
Mileidy Tavarez

Mileidy and Donni live in Tampa, Florida, and are raising four beautiful children – Milanni, Jethri, Malakai and Anaili. They have two babies in heaven.

Rosa's Words

Hi sister in Christ! By now, I am sure that God has spoken to your life in such a manner that you feel uplifted. I am happy that you picked up this book at this precise moment in your journey. God is always on time and He knew you needed to hear Landy's words. But I want to nudge another part of your heart: your marriage. A lot of times, we forget that it's not only our journey, but our husbands' too. Please put the book down and go grab him. He needs to read these words with you too. We will wait...

Now, I am going to say something that you may not want to hear, but stay with me. It may seem that we walk this journey alone, but our spouses walk with us. At times, we think it's only our journey because we are so immersed in our pain, that we allow our pain and sorrow to overshadow that of our spouse. My husband and I were no exception. I fell into the trap of not effectively communicating with Cassidy because I allowed my pain and sorrow to speak louder than my better judgment. Again, nobody is at fault. This is the reason I want to talk to you both about infertility and marriage.

These are topics that we don't like to bring up, because it's yet another part of life that we have to worry about. Still, I am going to ask you to do something hard. I want you to ask yourself, "When was the last time I opened my heart and truly told my spouse what I was feeling? When was the last time I spoke about the elephant in the room?" Now, get face-to-face with your spouse and ask him the same questions. Put this book down and have this conversation. Come back when you are ready to continue. We'll wait…

Our love story has really been straight out of the movies. I was that older, chubby girl, who thought that she would never find love. Then suddenly, I met this handsome, tall, kind man who would make me laugh all the time. It was love at first sight! I could not believe that I was the girl he chose as his wife. We got married ten months after our first date and immediately moved into our first home together. Life was perfect! We decided to start trying to have children immediately after marriage. This is when our challenging journey began.

After months of not being able to conceive, I began shutting Cassidy out of this important part of my life. He would try to talk to me, encourage me, and remind me of God's promises, but I would not listen. Instead, I spent hundreds of hours researching, looking into symptoms I thought I was experiencing, all because I needed to understand the causes of infertility. I allowed the what-ifs to overtake my mind. Feeling overwhelmed, scared, and alone, I was lost in my pain. All the while, the person who loved me the most, was sitting right next to me just wanting to love and remind me that everything was going to be okay. Does that not also sound like our Father in heaven? He constantly reminds us in Scripture that everything works out for those who love and believe in Him (Romans 8:28). He reminds us that everything will be alright, despite our pain, which tends to obstruct His voice.

Our desire to be parents is so near to our hearts that we don't know how to give it to Jesus. Be honest with yourself – does this sound like you? Ask your spouse, "Is this me? Do I do that?" Take a moment together to speak to God. With an open mind and heart, remind Him of your pain and give it completely to Him. Trust me, God can handle it. There's no rush! We will wait for you...

In a span of seventeen months, my husband and I lost three babies. During the loss, I would allow my husband to grieve with me. We would cry together and pray together. Every time, he would remind me of God's promise. I would silently nod my head and agree. Within a couple of weeks, I would go back to my old habits. These habits were blaming myself, being sad, and not talking about how I really felt with my husband. I knew Cassidy understood and loved me, but I wanted to be alone. His body was not the issue, it was mine. He was not the one struggling to become and stay pregnant – it was me. It was not him that just went through the physical pain of losing a baby; yes, that was me again. He wasn't the one that carried the baby in his womb, that was me. And he was not the one who felt that desire to be a mommy at the tender age of ten. I will ask: does this sound like you? Do you also keep your true feelings bottled up because of fear of what your husband might say or feel?

Wife: I am going to ask you to open that wound and talk about it with your spouse. Husband: no need to say a word, just listen. Don't worry, we have all the time in the world, we'll wait for you...

Cassidy's Words

To the husbands reading this story, you might be thinking, "How can I enter this situation without trying to "fix" anything or sound insensitive by oversimplifying what we observe?" Listening is essential. You see, listening is focusing on what your spouse is communicating without trying to come up with your "brilliant" masculine response. Listening to your wife makes her feel validated. Sometimes it may be helpful to just summarize what she said to show you are hearing her. When it is your turn to respond, try to communicate what you are feeling. Your wife will not see you as any less macho. This also reminds her that she is not alone in her feelings, which can create intimate bonding experiences.

One thing that is essential: do not try to mirror the emotions and feelings of your wife. Do not be afraid to express exactly what you are feeling even if you feel you are lacking the necessary emotions for the moment. Before childbirth, mothers and fathers do not have the same emotional experiences toward their baby because of the specific attachment prior to birth. The baby grows inside the mother; therefore, there is a special bond that the father cannot and will not experience. I am saying this so that you, as the husband, do not feel bad if there develops a disconnect in emotions between you and your wife, should there be a miscarriage or an inability to conceive. Your wife's emotions are not necessarily going to be your exact emotions at any given time. You are entitled to your own grief experience. "But what happens if there is a moment when I feel nothing?" you might ask. That is okay too. Never feel guilty for any of your feelings. It is important to remember this because there should not be any judgments concerning who is struggling with grief more. Now husband, talk to your wife. Wife: listen to what he has to say to you. Again, we will wait…

Rosa's Words

You might be asking yourself, "Why is Rosa speaking to me about my marriage when I *need* comfort on this journey of infertility?" The reason is that we cannot lose ourselves or our marriage while on this difficult journey. Sister, I know these are harsh words and I am sorry for that. I understand your desire to become a mom, with that monthly desperation for a positive pregnancy test, and all the steps you take to help maximize your chances. These are all valid feelings that keep us pushing forward and fighting for our dream. But don't lose sight of the blessings you have in front of you, namely your spouse and family. Although infertility has stolen our joy, our time, and our money, are we going to allow it to steal our marriage too?

For over three years, Cassidy and I tried to conceive. Three times we were successful but would lose the pregnancy. The first loss occurred at five and a half weeks, the second at nine weeks and three days, and the third at six and a half weeks. I now understand why King David, in his anguish, ripped off his clothes. The feeling of your body rejecting the child that you prayed and asked for is one that can't be put into words. Each time it happened, I felt numb, dead inside, and just broken. But by the grace of God, I survived my miscarriages. I am sorry if you have experienced that pain. The grief never fully goes away. Then again, I am not sure if I want the pain to go away, because it's a reminder of the immense love I have for my babies in heaven. Thank goodness for the love of God!

In my pain, I've also come to understand that God truly knows what is best for us. He works everything for our good. This includes those babies that are in heaven. The moment I truly just gave in and gave my infertility issues to God, became my turning point. I remember crying out, telling Him that I gave up. He could have my struggle with infertility because I didn't want it anymore. Immediately, I became a better wife to my husband, and was happier overall. Was it hard? Absolutely! Did I struggle to get to that point? You bet I did! But I got there. And sister, believe me when I say, you can too.

After countless doctor visits and thousands of dollars later, I was diagnosed with unexplained infertility. But little did I know that this situation was the point at which God would allow me to experience the "suddenly of God." I became naturally pregnant and, I might add, at the age of forty. My husband and I are expecting a baby girl in the Fall of 2020.

If I could have changed anything during my journey with infertility, it would be the way I communicated with my husband. Nevertheless, I am grateful that God was in the forefront of our marriage. I am also grateful that Cassidy is a man of God and was able to clearly see what was going on with me, allowing me to figure out my pain. But I wish I would have opened up more to my husband, reminding myself that as much as I needed him, he needed me too. You see, just as much as we have fought for our baby, we have had to fight for our marriage. Because of my despair, I asked my husband if he wanted a divorce, as I was not able to give him children. But I thank God for His love and grace! My husband reminded me that I was enough and that he loved me. I chose to believe him, whether we had children or not.

I have asked you to speak to your spouse on several occasions and to pray together. Now, I am going to ask you to look at each other and remind yourselves of the love you have for one another. While you are at it, pray together and rededicate your marriage and desire to be parents, to God, again. He listens because He really does care. Go ahead, we will wait...

I am so glad that you decided to open your heart and become vulnerable with each other. I will leave you with this: infertility is hard. It's not a journey for the weak. It's not a journey intended to be walked alone. And let's be honest! We don't have a Magic 8 Ball that tells us when the journey will be over. Walk it out with your spouse while affirming your love to each other, consistently communicating your thoughts and feelings. I assure you; it will get easier.

Your brother and sister in Christ,
Cassidy and Rosa

Cassidy and Rosa live in Ellenton, Florida. Cassidy manages the family business and Rosa works for a major health care provider. They both attend The Bridge Church in Bradenton, Florida.

CHAPTER ELEVEN

hurting husbands

(by Josue Feliciano)

To all the men out there struggling in silence, let me share a piece of my heart with you. Many times, we get hidden in the shadows of our wives' pain. Not realizing that we also hurt, we are often forgotten, and although it's unintentional, we've learned how to deal with it and process our pain separately.

When we lost our baby, I was heartbroken; I dealt with it in a different way. My wife did not understand why I wasn't grieving like her. The fact is, we all process our grief differently. I didn't talk about it nearly as much as she did, and at times, my lack of expression was mistaken for not caring. I was hurting and grieving, just not the way she expected. As men, it's difficult for us to express our feelings and be vulnerable, because we are expected to be the strong ones in the relationship. I had to be strong for my wife, who was a complete mess. I needed to keep it together for her, for us. I certainly couldn't just crumble!

When Landy told me the title of the book, *Silent Cries*, I could immediately relate to it. My cries were silent, my tears were hidden, and my suffering was suppressed. I was angry and felt helpless, with so many questions lingering like, *"Why me? Why us?"* I was a hurting husband who did not know how to process this foreign pain. My wife's feelings became a priority, while mine were tucked away.

As men, so many questions cross our minds: *"How do I help her? How should I console her? Am I not talking enough about it? Am I saying too much? Do I bring up the topic? What if she starts crying again? Is it too early to try again? Will she get offended?"* It's understandable that we'd have all these questions and potential scenarios running through our heads – we just don't want to add more pain to our wives' suffering. We want to see them happy again, which requires us to put on a brave face so that we can be there for them.

This was one of the toughest seasons of my life; I had never experienced a loss like this. I felt completely alone and had no one to talk to. I had to constantly remind myself that God was a good God and He was still in control. A couple verses that sustained me during this process was Psalm 34:18-19, which say, *"The Lord is close to the brokenhearted and saves those who are crushed in spirit. The righteous person may have many troubles, but the Lord delivers him from them all."* Although I dealt with loneliness during this time, God always provided the assurance that I was not alone.

Although we may not be as vocal or as expressive as our wives are, that does not negate the fact that we hurt. As difficult as it may be, I believe it's time for us men to start these conversations. When we express our feelings, we begin to experience freedom, which brings forth healing. Our wives need our support just as we need theirs. And if we lean on each other as a couple, we can heal together and become stronger as one.

My encouragement to all the husbands reading this is to allow yourself to feel what you feel, surrendering everything to God. Communicate with your wife and don't isolate yourself. Make yourself available to other men who have gone through the same thing. Although communicating feelings tends to come more natural for women, I believe it's just as important for us men to find ways to communicate our feelings with other men. There is power in community! Trust that God will place people in your path who will walk this journey with you. You don't have to do it alone.

From a man who understands you,
Josue Feliciano

CHAPTER TWELVE

---

women and their wombs

Infertility isn't something new. It originated in ancient times, and is documented throughout the Old and New Testaments, where we read of couples who struggled with barrenness. These were regular people with real feelings who were going through a painful season just like you and me. I don't know about you, but it's so encouraging to find women in the Bible who were feeling and thinking the same things we do today. And in each of their accounts, we get a glimpse not only at their journeys, but most importantly, how their stories ended.

You will find many similarities between these women and yourself. For this reason, it is a treat that their stories are found in the pages of the Bible. I'd like to think that this is a sweet reminder from our Heavenly Father that He loves and cares for us so much, that He intended to include these stories of faith in Scripture. Why would He do this? So that we can hold on tightly to His promises;

if He was able to do miracles for them, He can certainly do the same for us.

Abraham & Sarah
Genesis 15-21

This passage of Scripture contains one of the most well-known stories of infertility. In Genesis 17, Abraham and Sarah were promised a child, even though they were well beyond child-bearing years. God promised them a child and, twenty-five years later, that promise was fulfilled. Abraham was 100 years old and Sarah was 90 years old when Isaac was born.

When Sarah overheard the angel of God telling Abraham that he and his wife were having a child, she laughed. Sometimes God's plans seem absurd, and at times, laughable! But this is a lesson we should all learn, that when God speaks, He fulfills. This story is a true testament that there is nothing impossible for God.

Isaac & Rebekah
Genesis 25

It appears that history repeated itself with Isaac and Rebekah, as she would experience the same thing as her mother-in-law, Sarah. After marriage, Rebekah discovered that she could not conceive, after a long period of being barren. And so, after Isaac asked the Lord in prayer for a child, his prayer was answered! Rebekah's womb opened and they had twins – Esau and Jacob.

God surely knows how to give us double for our trouble, giving us more than what we could ever expect or imagine.

Jacob & Rachel
Genesis 29-30

Do you remember Jacob? His mother and grandmother were both barren. Well, guess what? His wife Rachel would experience the same thing. She was barren and became jealous of her sister Leah who was able to give Jacob children. Does this sound familiar? It's easy for us to become jealous of our sisters when they're having babies and we're not, especially when they have the blessing we crave. The story doesn't end there, however. Genesis 30:22 says, *"Then God remembered Rachel; He listened to her and enabled her to conceive."* God opened her womb and she was able to birth Joseph and Benjamin.

Just when it seems like God has forgotten about you, He reminds you that He hasn't. Just as He remembered Rachel, He remembers you!

Elkanah & Hannah
1 Samuel 1

Do you know that famous verse which couples use when posting their pregnancy announcements? You know, the one found in 1 Samuel 1:27. It says, *"For this child I prayed, and the Lord has granted me my petition which I asked of him."* Yes, that was Hannah's prayer. After praying for a son, Samuel was born, becoming the first prophet in Israel. Hannah had five more children.

This shows us that there is power in prayer. Just as Hannah prayed to the Lord and He granted her request, we can trust God with our prayers too. He listens and grants us our heart's desires.

Manoah & His Wife
Judges 13

Do you remember Samson, the strongest man to have ever lived? Well, he was a miracle baby. His mother, whose name is not revealed in the Bible, is known simply as Manoah's wife. She too was barren. One day, she received a visit from an angel telling her that she would conceive. And indeed, she did, becoming the mother of Samson.

God has different ways of speaking to his children. We just need to have an open heart to receive the Word He gives us. If we have the faith to believe it, God can make it happen.

The Shunammite Woman & Her Husband
2 Kings 4

The woman known as "the Shunammite" has an incredible story in Scripture. She had a beautiful servant-heart, preparing a room in her home for the Prophet Elisha to stay, whenever he would visit her town. This woman had everything, including a loving husband as well as money for a comfortable life. However, there was one thing missing – a child. And although she was barren, Elisha told her on one occasion that she would have a son within a year. This was a hard truth for her to accept, especially because she did not ask for it. The following year, Elisha's words were proved true when she had her baby boy.

The Bible says that even before we speak the word, God knows it. This woman had not revealed her desire to have a child, yet God, who knows our thoughts, knew what she wanted. You may not vocalize all your needs to those in your life but be encouraged that even when you don't say anything, God knows everything.

Zechariah & Elizabeth
Luke 1

This next couple was childless as well as old. And although the Book of Luke does not record Zechariah's prayer, we do know that the angel who visited him mentioned that he had prayed for a son. I think you would agree when I say that it's great when we pray for children, but it's so much sweeter when our husbands pray as well. This is exactly what Zechariah did. And as soon as he did, the angel appeared and promised him a son. Like Sarah, Zechariah could not believe it. He didn't think it would be possible. As a result, the angel told him that he would be mute until the fulfillment of the promise. With the passing of time, his wife Elizabeth gave birth to their son, John. A few days later, Zechariah's mouth was opened, and his tongue was set free to speak again. It's no wonder that his first words were praise to God!

This is a great reminder that God doesn't work based on our clock – His timing is not ours. This is hard to grasp, especially as women, because age does play a factor in our reproductive systems, which directly affects our ability to conceive. It's difficult to disregard our biological clock which does not stop ticking! Both Abraham and Sarah, along with Zechariah and Elizabeth, are here to remind us that age is nothing but a number. Listen to me! No matter how old you are or how long you have been struggling with infertility, time does not affect God's clock. He is able to open your womb and give you a child regardless of your age or the difficulty of your situation. There is absolutely nothing impossible for Him! If you doubt me, just use these stories to remind yourself of His power and faithfulness. He can surely do it again.

CHAPTER THIRTEEN

standing in faith

The only way we can stand in faith is if we stand on Scripture. The Bible says in Romans 10:17 that *"Faith comes by hearing and hearing the Word of God."* So, it's important to read the Word and constantly meditate on it because on that foundation, our faith is built.

We are already under a lot of stress, as the world around us may not be looking so bright according to our natural eyes. Therefore, we need to cling to our eternal hope, which is found in Jesus, embracing all the promises that He has for us in this precious book called the Bible. My hope is that you absorb these verses and make them your own. Out of countless Scriptures, I've selected a few that will enrich us and bring fulfillment to our souls.

Then God remembered Rachel; He listened to her and enabled her to conceive. *Genesis 30:22*

There will be no miscarriages or infertility in your land, and I will give you long, full lives. *Exodus 23:26*

You will be blessed above all the nations of the earth. None of your men or women will be childless, and all your livestock will bear young. *Deuteronomy 7:14*

For this child I prayed, and the Lord has granted me my petition which I asked of him. *1 Samuel 1:27*

Yet you brought me out of the womb; you made me trust in you, even at my mother's breast. From birth I was cast on you; from my mother's womb you have been my God. *Psalm 22:9-10*

The Lord is close to the brokenhearted and saves those who are crushed in spirit. The righteous person may have many troubles, but the Lord delivers him from them all. *Psalm 34:18-19*

They will have no fear of bad news; their hearts are steadfast, trusting in the Lord. *Psalm 112:7*

He gives the childless woman a family, making her a happy mother. Praise the Lord! *Psalm 113:9*

Children are a gift from the Lord; they are a reward from him. *Psalm 127:3*

For you created my inmost being; you knit me together in my mother's womb. I praise you because I am fearfully and wonderfully made; your works are wonderful I know that full well. *Psalm 139:13-14*

Before I formed you in the womb, I knew you, before you were born, I set you apart; I appointed you as a prophet to the nations. *Jeremiah 1:5*

You will keep in perfect peace those whose minds are steadfast because they trust in you. Trust in the Lord forever, for the Lord, the Lord Himself, is the Rock eternal. *Isaiah 26:3-4.*

But those who hope in the Lord will renew their strength. They will soar on wings like eagles; they will run and not grow weary they will walk and not be faint. *Isaiah 40:31*

So do not fear, for I am with you; do not be dismayed, for I am your God. I will strengthen you and help you, I will uphold you with my righteous right hand. *Isaiah 41:10*

I can do all things through Christ who strengthens me. *Philippians 4:6-8*

Do not be anxious about anything, but in every situation, by prayer and petition, with thanksgiving, present your requests to God. And the peace of God, which transcends all understanding, will guard your hearts and your minds in Christ Jesus. Finally, brothers and sisters, whatever is true, whatever is noble, whatever is right, whatever is pure, whatever is lovely, whatever is admirable—if anything is excellent or praiseworthy—think about such things. *Philippians 4:13*

Three times I pleaded with the Lord to take it away from me. But he said to me, "My grace is sufficient for you, for my power is made perfect in weakness." Therefore, I will boast all the more gladly about my weaknesses, so that Christ's power may rest on me. That is why, for Christ's sake, I delight in weaknesses, in insults, in hardships, in persecutions, in difficulties. For when I am weak, then I am strong. *2 Corinthians 12:8-10*

Being strengthened with all power according to his glorious might, so that you may have great endurance and patience, and giving joyful thanks to the Father, who has qualified you to share in the inheritance of his holy people in the kingdom of light. *Colossians 1:11-12*

Every good and perfect gift is from above, coming down from the Father of the heavenly lights, who does not change like shifting shadows. *James 1:17*

Cast all your anxiety on Him because He cares for you. *1 Peter 5:7*

CHAPTER FOURTEEN

stop the silence

As I sit on my couch at 3:08 AM typing these last few lines to end this book, I can't help but think, "Wow! I finally finished it." This was a project I began working on years ago but kept putting it off, because it was just too painful to produce. I began writing *Silent Cries* back in 2016, but so much has happened since then that many times I thought it was easier to tuck it away and just be silent. I had so many excuses as to why I couldn't finish it; most of them seemed good, like, "I am just too busy."

Now that the entire world has come to a standstill due to Covid-19 and the global pandemic we are currently facing, everyone is pretty much homebound. This seemed like the perfect opportunity to finish what I had started so long ago; it was time to stop the silence. And I hope this book has encouraged you to stop the silence as well. You don't have to live in silence any longer! Find your voice and speak up. Do it for you, do it for her, do it for them.

I don't know what will happen in the next few months or even in the next few years. But one thing I do know is that God is still writing my story. Although I thought this area of my life would finally produce a period, I have only reached a comma. But He is the Author and Finisher of my story, and I'm excited to see where this all ends. According to statistics, approximately one in eight couples or 12% of married women are affected by infertility in the United States. That's about 6.7 million people each year who have trouble conceiving or sustaining a pregnancy. Although I am one of the "one-in-eight," I have placed my faith in the One who has the power to do something great. I want you to be excited for your future as well, even if it doesn't look bright right now. In Jeremiah 29:11, the Lord declares, *"For I know the plans I have for you, plans to prosper you and not to harm you, plans to give you hope and a future."* In light of such a promise, you don't have to be scared to dream about your future, because God has a wonderful plan for your life. You can be hopeful again! Allow Him to reveal it to you so that your eyes can see it.

Ephesians 3:20 reminds us that, *"God is able to do exceedingly abundantly above all that we ask or think, according to the power that works in us."* I don't know about you, but I am believing for Him to do more than what I have ever asked or imagined. He has the power and ability to do it in both your life and mine. Friend, I stand in agreement with you today in asking our Heavenly Father for His perfect will to be done in your life. I cannot wait to hear the wonderful things He has for you! I am praying and rooting for you. I truly believe your best years are ahead and not behind you

Before I sign-off, promise me that you will use your voice to help others who are suffering in silence. For such a time as this, God is calling you to *be the one*.

Your friend,
Landy

CHAPTER FIFTEEN

share your story

This is a space where you can be vulnerable and transparent with yourself. True healing begins with being honest with yourself. I pray that as you journal your thoughts, you will begin to find your voice in the midst of your silent cries.

Acknowledgments

First and foremost, I would like to thank my Lord and Savior, Jesus Christ. I honestly didn't think I would ever finish this book; it was just too painful. But He gave me the courage and the strength to complete it.

Josh, what a journey we've been on! Thanks for being my rock and encouraging me to push forward in writing this book. Sharing our story hasn't been easy, but you've been so supportive, and for that I am grateful!

My parents, Pastors Enrique and Eny Perez. You guys are my biggest cheerleaders and my inspiration. Thank you for never losing hope and for your continual prayers.

My sister Kenia, your faith is admirable, and I tell you this all the time. I love how you believe without a shadow of a doubt that there is truly nothing impossible for God. Thank you for always reminding me that our God is greater!

Sabrina, my childhood friend! I'm honored that you would be a part of this project. Your journey has not been an easy one and I know your story will bring a lot of hope to all the beautiful women out there who await their miracle. Thank you!

Miledy, thank you for your consistency and for never forgetting about how I was doing even when time had passed or when everything looked "normal." You helped me process and deal with my loss with such care and grace.

Rosa, you truly get me! Although we've been friends for years, this season has brought us closer than ever. Our stories are similar, and we were able to encourage each other through our losses. I'm so thankful for you.

To my friends and family, and the army of prayer warriors...thank you for your prayers, words of encouragement, and your overall support. I love you all!

About the Author

Landy Perez-Feliciano is an author, speaker, and blogger. She debuted her first book in Spanish, *Un Momento de Silencio* and later translated it into English, *A Moment of Silence*. She loves to blog and inspire readers through her writings.

Landy and her husband Josh married in 2010 and live in Tampa, Florida. They both serve as youth pastors at their local church, La Senda Antigua.

Let's stay connected!

- Website: www.landypf.com
- Facebook: www.landypf.com
- Instagram: @landypf
- Twitter: @landypf

Printed in the United States
By Bookmasters